QuickBooks Online for Beginners 2022

The Most Updated Guide to QuickBooks for Small Business Owners

D1712933

Table of Contents

Introduction

QuickBooks is an accounting program that helps you manage your company's finances. Despite its small size, it has significantly impacted the accounting software industry with its handy evolution over the years, including reviews of QuickBooks' new features and functionality to accommodate small businesses best. QuickBooks is the ideal application for managing your financial activities when starting a small business.

You can easily start and run a small business without dealing with additional accounting issues. When combined with monitoring client information, sales, and transactions, it becomes a complete solution for small and medium-sized businesses.

With this book tutorial, you'll be able to set up your QuickBooks online in no time by entering your company's information into the dashboard and creating entries for vendors, customers, and payroll. You will also learn how to create customer-facing financial reports and how to file your taxes on time with the help of this book. You will be able to keep track of the progress of your company's operations and financial performance by using this.

Chapter 1: All About QuickBooks Online

How Does It Work?

It is common practice in small businesses to use double-entry accounting because it can help you manage your financial operations better and increase your company's flexibility in the face of market fluctuations. Every transaction in QuickBooks has two sides: "debits" on one side and "credits" on the other, and they all add up to the same total. In accounting terminology, this is referred to as "double-entry accounting." In most cases, QuickBooks will handle all of the data entry for you. If you give the client a bill for the products or services you provided, the consumer is obligated to pay you money. QuickBooks keeps track of credit card transactions and delinquent invoices from customers under accounts receivable. The sale proceeds are deposited into an income account, which is then closed as proof of the sale's proceeds. The direct deposit account is debited when a client uses direct deposit to pay you. When the payment is received, a credit is applied to your receivables account. Because the consumer no longer owes you money, your accounts receivable is reduced. Looking at this example, it's simple to see how a credit or debit can affect account balances.

Benefits of QuickBooks Online

1. QuickBooks Online is a popular choice for accountants and small business owners because it can be accessed anywhere and on almost any device. You will need an internet connection because the software and your data are saved on Intuit servers in the cloud, accessible from anywhere.

2. QuickBooks Online can also be set up to generate invoices for billable time and expenses for each transaction and provide quick email reports that go along with the transactions.

3. QuickBooks Online Plus is required for inventory monitoring. Nonetheless, some inventory bells and whistles found in the desktop software are missing in the Plus version. If QuickBooks Online's inventory capabilities

do not meet your needs, another option is to subscribe to a third-party inventory program.

4. Progress invoices are features available in QuickBooks Online Plus and allow you to track task expenditures and profitability. On the other hand, sales orders are not supported by QuickBooks Online.

5. Intuit releases new QuickBooks Online features and enhancements every month. As a result, the boundaries between online and offline are blurring. Try QuickBooks Online for free for 30 days to see if the software meets your requirements.

However, based on the advantages listed, QuickBooks online is unquestionably the best option. The confusion now revolves around selecting the best versions for accounting activities that meet your bookkeeping requirements and budget.

Versions of QuickBooks

There are several factors to consider when developing an effective bookkeeping system:

- While on the QuickBooks page, select "Plans & Pricing." QuickBooks Online provides several options.
- Small businesses can use Simple Start, Plus, or Advanced, whereas independent contractors can use Self-Employed.

QuickBooks Online Self-Employed

This is the version with the fewest features. Users can access basic reports as well as income and expense tracking. These features include processing and printing checks, extremely simple invoicing, and a few designed reports to streamline bookkeeping processes. On the other hand, this version restricts data access to a single user at a time.

QuickBooks Online Plus

QuickBooks Online Plus has quickly become the most popular option with over a million users. Up to five people can use the system simultaneously and have complete control over their data while allowing for full bill management and payment, time tracking, and inventory tracking.

QuickBooks Online Advanced

QuickBooks Online's advanced edition includes batch invoices and spending, company analytics, and premium care, but it costs more per month than the Plus edition. If you're unsure, QuickBooks Plus is your best bet. If you require complex accounting knowledge, you could upgrade to Online Advanced.

Chapter 2: Getting Started

How to Get Started with QuickBooks Online

QuickBooks' interface, particularly the home screen, is genuinely user-friendly. QuickBooks Plus is the entry-level edition for small businesses, including essential features. QuickBooks is available on a variety of platforms.

In the address bar of your preferred browser, such as Chrome or Mozilla Firefox, type "https://quickbooks.intuit.com/au/." If you have never used QuickBooks before, you must first create an account.

Sign in with your user ID, password, and other relevant information by clicking the button in the upper right corner of the screen and selecting QuickBooks Online.

After you sign in, you will have access to various features. QuickBooks Online provides security alert notifications, which provide a warning when a transaction exceeds the limits set by the company's manager.

The homepage is displayed after successfully signing in. On one side of the page, there are some interesting features about the company, such as activities, sales, and purchase journal entries. Another section contains the Open Item report, a table displaying information about customer name, vendor name, account description, and amount.

The "New" button in the top right corner of the screen allows quick access to creating new transactions and other records. In contrast, the Search feature, built into this cloud app, allows users to find specific transactions by entering values of their choice.

Advanced Search: This provides more detailed options for finding a product/service, such as customer name, vendor name, transaction type, and more.

Recent Transactions: This feature allows the user to search for transactions by date and amount that occurred within a specific time frame.

Show Less: This displays a list of all transactions sorted by date, as well as quick access options for updating and marking highlighted transactions as hidden or visible.

You can collapse the window by clicking the hamburger icon, which reveals options for canceling or completing a transaction, as well as access to the full-screen menu.

How to Add Customers

Client names will appear on invoices and other forms created with this option. The Itemized receipt to the section below in QuickBooks automatically reflects what you type here.

1. At the top, click on the "Customers" menu.
2. From the dropdown menu, choose "Customer Center".
3. Choose "New Customer". In the dropdown menu and fill in the required details.
4. Click "Okay" to save the changes.

How to Add Products

An invoice may include the products you sell and the discounted prices displayed on the product. It is important to note that an inventory item is not the same as a required sales tax. QuickBooks supports multiple entries as well as descriptions of the transaction's items. To add an item to your Item list, do the following:

1. Choose the command "Lists Item." QuickBooks' item list window will appear.
2. To access the item menu, click the "Item" button in the lower-left corner of the item list window.

3. Press the "New" button. When you press this, QuickBooks will open the "New Item" box.

4. Using the boxes in the new item window, describe the product you want to add. The first step is to decide what kind of product you want to include. QuickBooks includes additional description boxes.

5. After you've finished filling out the fields in the new item window, click "Okay." QuickBooks adds the item to the item list immediately after you describe it.

How to Manage Users

If a small business grows, it may add more QuickBooks users. The standard user and business admin, on the other hand, have complete and unrestricted access to QuickBooks. In contrast, the report and time track have limited access to certain QuickBooks files and functionalities. This means that if you add more users to your QuickBooks business, you'll need to create separate sub-company files and assign edit rights to each of the users to administer rights based on their needs and responsibilities.

To manage a user's role or permissions, do the following:

1. Sign into QuickBooks with a user profile that can manage users.

2. Select "Settings" at the gear button

3. Select "Manage Users".

4. Choose the user to be edited.

5. In the "User Type" dropdown menu, select the "New User" type. This section has four types of users: standard, company type, time tracking, and reporting.

6. Select the "User Settings".

7. Select "Save".

How to Add A Service

To create an accurate record of your activity, transactions should include all information and services. The fields for items and services that can be imported are listed below. A more detailed overview of the fields can be found by manually inserting product and service items.

Before beginning a transaction, a chart of accounts must be created with the Product/Service name, price/rate, income account, and quantity as-of-date. The steps for adding a service in QuickBooks are as follows:

1. Click on "Products and Services" to access the product and services list in the left menu bar.

2. Click on the "New" button in the upper right corner of the screen.

3. Select whether the item you are adding is inventory, a non-inventory product, a service, or a bundle of products or services.

4. Complete the information requested for the item type you are adding. Click "Save" and close.

How to Use Projects

The Projects feature in QuickBooks 2013 enables small-business owners to synchronize their financial data across multiple computers and even add more devices to their network, which was previously impossible. Not only can you better manage your finances and make them more transparent, but QuickBooks 2013 also allows you to enhance some of the functionality of your desktop program. Projects enable small business owners to keep track of their revenue, material costs, and labor costs. Here's an example of how to access the projects function in the QuickBooks dashboard:

1. Click on the "New Project" button over to the right.

2. Enter a project name in that field and select a customer from the dropdown list

3. Click "Save," and your new project will appear in a list on the "Projects" page account settings.

How to Check Your Company ID

This ID is used to access QuickBooks. It enables you to easily access your business, restore data, and perform other accounting tasks online. This could be an issue if you have many company files or QuickBooks accounts. A solid ID will assist you in finding a file among a terabyte of data.

The steps to check your ID in QuickBooks are as follows:

1. Navigate to the "Account and Settings" tab by clicking the setting icon.
2. Click on the "Billing & Subscriptions" section. The business ID is shown at the top of the billing and subscription section.

How to Enter an Opening Balance for the Chart of Accounts.

The chart of accounts is a list of all your company's accounts, as well as their balances. When using QuickBooks, you can use these accounts to categorize your sales forms into reports and tax forms. Each account has a transaction history and is divided into several smaller accounts to make accounting easier for the user. QuickBooks automatically calculates your profit and loss accounts as you enter transactions into the system. This accounting feature consists of four major components: expense accounts, liabilities, income, and assets.

Here are the steps in entering an opening balance for the chart accounts:

1. In the left-hand menu, click "Accounting".
2. Then, click "Charts of Accounts" at the top of the page.
3. Next, scroll in the account you wish to set and select "Edit" in the dropdown arrow.
4. Enter the balance amount and the date you wish to apply, save and close.

Editing an Opening Balance for the Chart of Accounts

1. Navigate to "Settings" and then to "Chart of Accounts".
2. Locate the account and then click "View Registration".
3. Locate the balance entry that represents the opening balance. To find the opening balance item, sort the date column from latest to oldest.
4. Click on the "Opening Balance Entry".
5. Adjust the amount.
6. Click "Save".

Resetting Password

In case you are unable to log into your account:

1. Go to http://account.intuit.com/
2. Click "Sign In" at the top right.
3. Enter your sign-in credentials (email address and password), and you will go to the login page (www.qbo.intuit.com), scroll down just a bit, and click "Forgot my User ID or Password."
4. Enter your phone number, email, or user ID to receive a code.
5. After entering the information that QuickBooks needs to reset your password, click on "Reset".
6. Key in the 6-digit code sent to your email or phone, depending on your choice. When prompted to replace your security question, just click "Okay".
7. Complete the following prompts to retrieve your password or reset it.

How to Change Your Company Settings

The Company tab allows you to view information such as the company's name, address, contact information, and Employer Identification Number (EIN). Adjustments may be made to meet both users' and customers' needs on the accounts. These changes can be made from various tabs, including Billing & Subscription, Usage, Sales, Expenses, Payments, Time, and Advanced. You can change your company's settings by following the steps outlined below.

To change settings:

1. Click "Settings".
2. Navigate to the "Account and Settings" section.
3. Click on a tab.
4. In a section, click "Edit".
5. Choose an item to edit. A field emerges, prompting you to make changes, then save.
6. Click "Done" to save your changes.

How to Record A Journal Entry

Accounting journals are necessary because they track how money is spent; it would be difficult to determine where funds were spent without them. Accounting may appear to be the last thing you want to do while running a small business, but accounting is not complex mathematics; rather, it is the process of capturing and logically presenting financial data. Journaling is the same thing.

1. Click the "New" button to access the accounting field for new entries.
2. Click on the "Journal Entry" tab.

3. Select an account depending on credit or debit needs, then key in the data in the appropriate column and format.
4. Depending on the choice of the transaction, enter the same amount on the opposite side, either credit or debit the account. Countercheck to ensure both the credit column and the debit column balance on one line.
5. In the note area, provide the reason for the journal entry.
6. Click "Save" and close.

Chapter 3: Invoicing and Quoting Tutorials

How to Create an Invoice in QuickBooks

How do you get paid for the goods and services you offer?

After-sales, you may want to send an invoice to your customers. Simply include the products or services you are selling on an invoice and email it to your client. QuickBooks facilitates this transaction by creating invoices for each transactional activity in your company.

The following are the steps for creating an invoice:

1. Create an invoice from scratch.

2. Select the "Create Invoices" option on the "Customers" menu.

3. Select a customer or customer job from the dropdown menu.

4. Select "Add New" to include customers not listed.

5. Input the relevant information at the top of the form.

6. Select the item(s) in the detail field.

Create a Discount Item

1. Go to the "Lists" menu on the home screen.

2. Click on the "Item List" option.

3. Select "New."

4. Select the "Type Discount" from the dropdown menu.

5. Input an item name or number and a brief description of the product or service.

6. Enter the discount amount and/or percentage in the amount field.

7. Choose the income account you want to use to track discounts you give to customers from the account dropdown menu.

8. Click on a "Tax Code" for the item.

9. Select "Okay", "Save", then "Close".

Creating and Sending an Invoice in QuickBooks

Creating and sending an invoice is the foundation of any transaction because customers and small business owners must share the details for accounting purposes and customer payment processing. The steps for creating and sending invoices in QuickBooks are as follows:

1. Click on the "Create Invoices" on the homepage or the customer menu on the QuickBooks dashboard.
1. Click on the "Job Tab" on the customer menu, then choose customer for estimate window to appear.
2. Select the "Estimate" to be included in the invoice
3. Then, click on "Save" and close.

Editing an Invoice in QuickBooks

It is possible to make mistakes during the entry process. To change or edit an invoice, follow the steps outlined below:

1. Click on the "Invoice" you wish to edit.
2. Choose the "Edit" options dropdown from the invoices box.
3. Delete the existing payment on QBO before pushing the updated invoice.

How to Customize an Invoice in QuickBooks

A personalized invoice allows you to sell your company and promote your brand. The invoice logo represents your company's brand and appears on all transaction forms in QuickBooks Online. Because your logo will be created outside of QBO, keep the following factors in mind when designing yours. The logo should be as follows:

1. A gif, bmp, png, jpg, jpe, or jpeg file less than 10 MB in size.
2. Bit depth of twenty-four bits or less (or color depth).
3. Either square or round.

Customizing an invoice, assigning tax codes to goods, assigning pricing to things, generating an item for a product, and documenting hardware and software purchases inventories are some of the most common modifications in the QuickBooks system.

These changes are affected by the following steps:

1. To begin, go to the "Gear" icon in the top right-hand corner.
2. Choose "Custom Form Styles" from the "Your Company" dropdown menu.

3. Choose "Invoice" from the "New Style" dropdown menu. This panel has three tabs: Design, Content, and Emails.

    Design – This is where you can change or add your logo, as well as your font and color scheme.

    Content – This is where you can change your content, add a website/address, and change the label sizes.

    Emails – This is where you can choose whether to show complete or partial data and write a note for your client. Most of your work will be stored in the "Content" tab.

You can customize what information appears in your header in the first editing area. Mark any of the boxes to remove a field.

In the middle section, you can change the columns, add items, and add descriptions. You can also display the total amount owed to a client and payments and credits.

You can customize the third party with a statement and tagline and any discount, deposit, or estimate options.

Finally, double-check that the email you sent matches the invoice you received. This invoice template is now finished and ready to use. Each option is described in detail to easily create a professional invoice.

How to Delete an Invoice in QuickBooks

An invoice may need to be deleted if it has been duplicated or if the transactions have been canceled for various reasons. The following is the procedure for deleting an invoice:

1. Click on the "Sales" or "Expenses" menu to find the transaction.
2. Click on the dropdown tab and choose "View" or "Edit" to access the transactions.
3. You can also add the reasons for the deletion or cancellation on the memo area then save the details.
4. Choose more in the footer, then delete.
5. Click "Yes" to effect the changes.

How to Print an Invoice in QuickBooks

Invoices can be printed for distribution to customers or financial reporting. If this is the case, follow the steps below to create a copy.

1. Select "Reports" on the panel on the left.
2. Type "Transactions List by Vendor" on the search bar.
3. Click on the correct date under the "Report" period.
4. Select "Run Report" to print.

How to Set Up Auto-Invoice Reminders

If a customer does not pay an invoice by the due date, they are reminded via invoice reminders. When you enable invoice reminders for the first time, default reminders are set. You can change or remove these reminders to meet your organization's needs.

To set up automatic invoice reminders:

1. Navigate to the "Account and Settings" menu under "Settings".
2. Click the "Sales" tab.
3. Select "Edit" from the "Reminders" menu.
4. Activate the "Automatic Invoice Reminders" feature.
5. Choose "Reminder 1" from the menu and flip it on.
6. Specify the days and times before or after from the dropdown menu. There is a 90-day grace period for sending invoice reminder emails.
7. You may add more reminders as necessary.
8. After enabling reminders, you may modify the message. Note that you may adjust each reminder's email template to meet the preset dates.
9. Edit the topic line as required in the "Subject" line area.

10. To customize your welcome, tick the "Use Email Greeting" option. Choose an appropriate salutation from the provided menus.

11. In the email message field, delete the text and write your own. You may also use the standard message.

12. After that, tap "Save and Done".

How to Manage Overdue Invoices in QuickBooks

As a businessperson, a consistent flow of funds in and out is critical in any company to enable smooth day-to-day operations. Unpaid invoices can cause a slew of problems for your business. The first step in informing your customers that they have a payment obligation is to send them past-due notices. Another strategy for assisting your customers in making timely payments is to offer them online payment options.

The steps for dealing with past-due debts are outlined below:

1. Click on the "Customer" menu

2. Choose the option of "Receiving Payments".

3. Select the client from the dropdown menu under "Received From".

4. Set the amount to be settled by adding it in the "Payment Amount" area.

5. Save and exit the program.

6. Click on the "Okay" button to continue.

How to Track Billable Time in QuickBooks

If you bill by the hour or pay people based on the number of hours they work, tracking billable time is ideal. In this instance:

1. Enter the job as a "Sub-customer" of the customer to track billable time.

2. Click the "Sale" or "Invoice" tab to choose the customer.

3. Select "New" customer.

4. Enter all the appropriate details for the "Sub-customer."

5. Click the "Sub-customer Check Box".

6. Select the parent customer in the "Parent Customer" dropdown menu.

7. Click the "Bill" button with a parent.

8. Select "Save".

Activate Billable Time

1. Select "Account Settings" from the dropdown menu under "Settings."

2. Select the "Time" tab from the dropdown menu.

3. In the timesheet, choose "Edit" from the context menu.

4. Select "Allow Time to be Billable" from the menu.

5. To allow users to observe billable rates, click the "Show Billing Rate for Users Entering the Time" option when entering the time.

6. Click "Save," then click "Done" to complete the process.

Recording Billable Time

1. Click on the "Time" tab, then select "Time Entries".

2. Choose the "Add Time" option and the appropriate user.

3. Customize the date ranges, then choose the day(s) entries are done for.

4. Input the hours worked or press the "Start and End Date" tab to add the date ranges.

5. Select "Add Work" details, then select the client or the project from the dropdown menu.

Chapter 4: Sales and Receipts

How to Record A Refund

The customer's money should be refunded, and the books should be balanced to ensure that the transaction's reflections are documented. This section explains how to record a refund based on various factors, such as whether the client has paid or issued the invoice to the correct individual.

1. To begin, click "New" and then "Credit Memo."
2. Select a suitable client in the customer field.
3. Add the credit memo, date of amount, tax, and product or service (if applicable).
4. Close it by clicking "Save".

5. Assuming the consumer has overpaid, the credit message is unneeded.

6. Select "Expense" from the "New" dropdown menu.

7. Enter the appropriate client in the "Payee" section.

8. In the Payment account area, pick the refunding bank.

9. Select the debtor's account in the "Category" section

10. Enter the refund amount in the "Amount" field.

11. Select the applicable tax in the "Tax Box", including the inclusive and exclusive tax.

12. To save your work, click "Save."

13. Then, choose to receive money from the "New" menu.

14. Fill in the payment method and a deposit amount for the client. The balance should be zero since they cancel each other.

15. Click "Save" and close it.

16. Match the record found in your online banking for verification

Refund for Paid Bills

1. Select "New", then pick "Client Credit" from the dropdown option.

2. Input the payment date, amount, tax, and category columns for the transactions you will get credit.

3. Select "Save" and then click "Close".

4. Add the payee, choose the "Client Credit", and deposit methods from the dropdown menus.

Credit Card Refunds

1. Click "New" and then "Credit Card" from the dropdown menu.

2. Choose the applicable client in the "Payee" field.

3. Input the payment date, the amount of the refund, the tax, and the category.

4. Choose "Save and Finish" to complete your refund.

How to Create A Receipt

QuickBooks can create and track sales receipts. You will provide customers with an immediate sales receipt when you charge customers for future remittances. This QuickBooks feature reduces errors, saves time, and reduces the likelihood of recurring conflicts. It saves time by eliminating the need to enter receipt data twice. Here's how to make a receipt in QuickBooks:

1. Click the "New" tab from the dropdown list.

2. Click either the "Refund Receipt" or the "Give Refund" options from the dropdown menu.

3. Choose the client to be repaid from the dropdown menu by clicking on the "Customer" option.
4. Click the "Refund" option
5. Select the bank into which payments were deposited from the dropdown option.
6. Add all returning items or services to the "Product or Service" column.
7. Fill in the appropriate boxes for the date, quantity, rate, amount, and tax, then click "Save" and close.

How to Receive A Payment

Using a sales receipt or a bank deposit to pay an invoice counts revenue twice but leaves the invoice unpaid. As a result, collection operations may become ineffective, and client relationships deteriorate. Receiving payments and adjusting amounts in accounting is thus just as important as collecting money. Follow these steps to ensure that payments are received and that the charts of accounts are accurate.

1. To access, click the "Receive Payment" button.
2. At the top of the left menu bar, click the "New" button.
3. Under "Customers", choose "Receive Payment" in the top column. It is critical to apply the received money to the relevant customer invoice.

4. To find the correct invoice, choose the client in the top-right corner of the receiving payment page. Choose the client from whom you got money.

5. Enter the date you received your payment.

6. Choose between a check or cash as your payment option.

7. If cash was received, provide the check number, or leave it blank if not received.

8. Choose the proper bank account into which the cheque should be deposited.

9. Enter the total amount of cash or checks received.

10. Enter the percentage of the total cash collected in "F" that will be applied to each invoice mentioned in "G".

11. Click the green "Save and Close" button to save the transaction.

12. Hover over "Sales" after selecting "Customers" from the left menu.

13. Locate the client whose payment you logged in and click on their name.

14. Check to see whether the invoice for which payment was received has been recorded as "Paid."

15. Check that the payment is indicated as "Closed." If payment is displayed as "Open," it has not been properly applied to an invoice.

Chapter 5: Bank Accounts

How to Connect to Your Bank Account

With the current digitization of the banking industry, most transactions are done online, with banks embracing this technology to keep up with the current dynamics and ensure a wider reach. QuickBooks' features and settings allow you to connect to your bank accounts and monitor transactions as they occur.

1. On the homepage's "Bank Accounts" section, click "Connect an Account".
2. Select a bank and a username and password for account access.

3. When finished, click "Log In". Once connected, you will get a list of all your bank accounts.

4. Select the business account and notify QuickBooks of its existence. QuickBooks will download all transactions for the preceding 90 days with a single click.

5. Choose the "Category" or "Match" column on the "Bank and Credit Cards" tab to sort the transactions.

6. Click it to see the dropdown details for the first transaction in the list.

7. To re-categorize a transaction, use the transaction menu. Click "Add" in the column on the right.

8. Choose "Payee". Press on "Add New" to add a new payee to the menu.

9. Enter the new payee's name and click "Save". After that, you may fill in the blanks.

10. Open the transaction and choose "Transfer". Purchases from various categories might be divided.

11. In the "Split Transaction" box, choose the relevant categories and their respective amounts.

12. Go to "Batch Actions" and click "Accept" to accept all of them.

13. Click the "In QuickBooks" tab, pick the transaction, and undo any wrong entry. Once in "New Transactions", you may relocate it.

How to Import A Spreadsheet of Transactions

In this case, we'll assume you used a personal credit card for both personal and business expenses. You then downloaded the transactions from your credit card company as an Excel document and deleted all non-business-related transactions. You will be given an Excel file containing business transactions that you can import into QuickBooks. The steps for importing are as follows:

1. Remove the extraneous data from the excel file to clean it up.
1. To make the XLS file readable by QuickBooks, convert it to CVS format by choosing "File" and "Save As" and setting the file type to CSV.
2. Select the account the file is to be added on
3. To upload the file, go to the "Accounts" page and click on the account to be added.
4. In the top right-hand corner of the screen, click the downward-pointing arrow next to the "Updated" button.
5. Select the "File Upload" option from the dropdown menu
6. QuickBooks will ask you where you got your data from on the next page, whether it's a file on our computer or an upload directly from our financial institution.

7. Select the QuickBooks account where you want to upload the bank file. It is not always necessary to assign an existing registration; you can always "Add New" and create a new account for your needs.

8. The data in each column should be interpreted and mapped into a transaction. Each QuickBooks transaction has a date column, and each transaction in the excel spreadsheet has a date column. QuickBooks includes a description box as well. Column 4, Memo, is the closest match to the description. Finally, and most importantly, the amount of the transaction.

9. Distinguish between the two types of bank transactions. Separate payments and deposits into separate columns. Remember that banks may combine all statistics into one column and use negative and positive values.

10. On the following page, click "Next," and QuickBooks will display all transaction data as it has been interpreted. You'll see the matching dates, descriptions, and sums, and if everything looks correct, you can continue with the import by clicking next.

11. Verify the transaction.

How to Set Up a Direct Bank Feed

Direct feeds connect your bank account to QuickBooks safely and dependably. QuickBooks can accept transactions without requiring you to enter your bank's sign-in credentials. This is accomplished by establishing a direct connection with the bank.

The following are the steps for enrolling in a direct bank feed:

1. Go to the "Banking Area".
2. Click the "Link Account" option in the top-right corner of the screen.
3. Enter your bank's name into the search field and click on it to find it.
4. Select the "Get Direct Bank Feeds" option and create a Client Authority Form.

Chapter 6: GST and BAS

The timely submission of your Firm Activity Statement is an important aspect of running a small business. When cash flow is tight, no one wants to make late payments.

Failure to file will result in fines and additional fees.

Setting Up a GST and BAS:

1. Select the "GST" option from the left-hand navigation menu.

2. Click "Get Started". This will display the Set-up BAS screen.

Your one-stop shop for everything BAS

Let's set up BAS so we can calculate GST and other obligations, prepare for lodgment, and you can even lodge BAS without leaving QuickBooks.

Get started

3. Choose the accounting method and BAS lodgment frequency appropriate for your business: monthly, quarterly, or annually.

4. Choose the appropriate BAS, PAYG Installments frequencies, and PAYG Withholding. If you require other tax reporting option-click, show other taxes, and click on "Relevant Tax".

5. Click "Save and Finish".
6. Click "Done".

How to Set Up GST Tracking and BAS E-Lodgment

The dashboard monitors and summarizes GST-recorded QuickBooks transactions. This provides a quick summary of how much you owe the tax office for a specific time. GST Rates are QuickBooks Online default codes used to code the applicable GST code against your transaction.

Set up a GST tracking and BAS e-lodgment system by following the steps below.

1. Click the "GST Centre" from the left-hand side navigation bar.
2. Compare your BAS figures to the report, BAS summary, BAS details, and amendment details.
3. Click on "GST" from the left menu.

4. Select "Prepare BAS Link" under the "Next BAS to Lodge" section.
5. The BAS window has been prepared to dominate BAS fields based on the values recorded against the Tax Codes for the selected period. During preparation, some fields may necessitate direct insertion.
6. Click the record to reveal a left-hand menu for adjustments.
7. Click "Mark as Lodged" and complete the BAS period.

How to Prepare and Lodge Your BAS

Other than the GST, some businesses are required to report taxes. PAYG withholdings and PAYG income tax installments are the most common additional taxes. Fringe benefits, fuel taxes, and luxury contexts are other taxes that can be avoided. By enabling the GST setup, you can report additional taxes. You can also enable them while accumulating GST or changing the GST settings. To enable in settings, follow the steps below:

1. Click on the "GST" tab from the left-hand navigation bar.
2. Select "Savings" and then "Tax Savings".
3. Tick the boxes next to the taxes you'll be reporting on, as well as the frequency, if applicable. Other taxes can be used to pay some additional taxes. There is no need to do anything else. QuickBooks is inventive, and it will assign

them to the appropriate accounts in the chart of accounts in a systematic manner.

4. When you're ready to file a BAS, go to the "GST Center" and choose "Prepare a BAS". Enter the total amount you must report for each tax. This will report them in the appropriate boxes automatically.

Chapter 7: Staff and Payroll

How to Set Up Payroll in QuickBooks

Setting up employee payroll in QuickBooks is simple; employees can not only view and download their pay stubs, but they can also enter their information.

All that is required is to send them an email inviting them to log in and enter information about the activity they have completed or the workforce before they are set up in QuickBooks.

Below are the steps to recording and reporting taxes:

1. Go to "Payroll", then click on "Employees".

2. Select "Add Employee", and then input the employee's name.

3. Check the section that enables workers to submit their personal information and access their payslips online using QuickBooks, and then enter the employee's email address.

4. On the invite employees page, click on "Invite Employees". The employees will get a link to QuickBooks Online Workforce to enter their personal information. This includes their name, gender, and birth date. They can also enter their address and work information.

5. QuickBooks will immediately add workers to the list of active employees after they have entered all the essential information, but the list will still display them as incomplete.

6. Add employment details such as payment schedule and payment history for every employee, tax information, and the workplace pension.

7. After you complete the form, click on "Save".

How to Add Employees

Gathering basic information on your workers, such as their name, date of birth, and current contact information, is necessary before you begin.

1. Employees can be found by selecting the "Employees Section" menu option.
2. If this is your first employee, add them to the list.
3. Fill in the employee's first and last name.
4. To begin, click "Add my Employee." Fill in the gender, date of birth, email, and employee's address.
5. Save your work and proceed to the next step.
6. Input the employee's payday, method of payment, and amount paid.
7. You will be asked to fill out various forms in the following field based on your response to whether the employee has been paid since you started.
8. Select "Save and Continue."

How to Process A Pay Run

After you've set up payroll in QuickBooks and added employees, you're ready to create a pay run. A pay run only needs to be set once for the date part, after which all subsequent pay runs will be moved to the next pay date period.

1. Go to the main payroll screen and click on "New Pay Run."

2. Once you open the pay run screen, select "Pay Schedule". Input the date for the pay period ending and when the pay run is paid, then click "Create".

3. Following the click of the create button, the next screen displays a summary of all employees in that run, including tax and their salaries or earnings. By clicking on the individual employee, you can view more information about them.

4. The action button is important because it allows you to make additional selections to correct or amend the employee pay run.

5. After making all the necessary changes, employees' full details can be hidden by clicking back on the employee's name.

6. Look for any warnings before completing the pay run. Click on it to get started.

7. After filling in the information needed, click "Save" and note any prompt alerts for an action.

8. To finish the pay run, click on "Finalize Pay Run" and verify that the date paid is correct, then click "Finalize."

9. Payslips can be sent to employees quickly using the payslip option.

10. After it has been finalized, the pay run is now locked. Only before any bank statements are processed can they be unlocked and changed.

11. Once the pay run is complete, download the files that will be uploaded to the bank, run any payroll reports, and send payslips.

How to Create Timesheets, Leave, and Expenses for Employees

Creating Employee's Timesheets

Employees who are required to use timesheets will be able to view, create, and delete timesheets on their own from within the Work Zone app.

Employees must use timesheets in the employee details, Pay Run defaults page, Payroll Settings, and Employee Portal Settings if they want to access timesheets in Work Zone.

1. Select the timesheet icon on the bottom of the screen.
2. Tap the timesheet area on the homepage.
3. Click on "Employees".
4. Click on the "Manage Employees" tab.
5. Select "Create a Timesheet".
6. Select the employee's name and select the week.

7. Select the "Work Time". Put the start time, end time, break taken, and their location/

8. Click "Save".

9. Click on "Manage Employees".

10. Select "Create Request" and choose the employee.

11. Select "Leave Category" and enter the period the employee will be on leave on the first and last days of the leave. The system will calculate and estimate the number of required leave days.

12. Click on "Approve Immediately".

Creating Expenses for Employees

1. Click on "Manage Employees".

2. Click on "Create Expense Request".

3. Select the employee and the description of the expense being paid for

4. Input the expense date, the category, and the location. You can add a note choosing the tax code and the amount of the expense.

5. You can add an attachment that can be in the form of a pdf.

6. You can click on approve immediately or leave it empty and click on the "Create" button.

7. Now your expense request will reflect on the next payroll.

How Employees Can Self Service

If an employer grants access to the portal, the employee will be instructed to activate their account and log in.

Follow these steps to activate your account:

1. To begin, open the email inbox associated with the email address that you provided to your employer.
2. Find and open the email with the subject line "Login Information for Your Company Payroll."
3. To create a password, click on the link in the email you received.
4. Return to your email inbox and locate the email with the subject line "User Account Created."
5. In this email, you will be provided with the username for your portal account. This is the username for which you have created a password.
6. Click the email link that directs to the employee dashboard, which will take you to the login page.
7. To access the self-service portal, log into the portal using the password and the username
8. You now have access to the self-service portal. It is necessary to bookmark the login page for easy access to the portal in the future.

How to Reset Your Password

If you have forgotten your password for the ESS Portal, follow the steps below to reset it.

1. Go to the "Employee Self-Service Portal" and log in.
2. Select "Forgotten Password" on the login page.
3. Enter your email address and select "Recover Password."
4. A reset prompt will be sent to the email address provided during the signup.
5. Open the email and select the link to reset your password.
6. Create a new password and enter it a second time to confirm the password.
7. Select "Set Password."
8. Select the link to log back into the portal.
9. Enter your email and new password to log in.

The Work Zone App for Employees

Work Zone integrates with QuickBooks payroll, allowing employees to access self-service on their Android or iOS device.

Setting Work Zone App for Employees

1. Download work zone from google play store or iOS.

2. Enter the email address and password to log in to access your employee service portal.

3. Create a pin that you will use each time you open the app.

Getting Around the Work Zone

To access the menu, click the hamburger icon. You can do a variety of things from here, including:

- Log out of the app.
- View login settings in the gear button.
- View own personal payroll details on employees list.
- View the business access.

Contents on the Home Screen

- Any content which requires employee acknowledgment.
- Leave balances.
- The last payslips.
- Timesheet.
- Expense summary
- Next shift time.

Contents on the Profile Icon

- Employee details.
- Bank account.

- Payment summaries.
- Super funds.
- Leave.
- Emergency contacts.
- Other documents.

If you log out of the app, you will be prompted to enter your email address, password, and PIN to re-enter it. If you exit the app and return later, you will only need to enter your PIN.

Enabling Work Zone

This feature is not enabled by default. You will enable it in the business portal so that employees can use it from their smartphones. You must navigate to "Payroll Settings" and then "Employee Portal Settings".

The first step is to decide whether employees will be able to clock in and out using "Work Zone". The sub-settings are optional, but they will affect the employee workflow when clocking in and out. The following settings must be used:

1. When employees clock in or out, take photos of them.
2. Allow employees to log in with a higher classification.
3. Allow employees to use scheduled start and finish times when clocking in and out.

4. Send reminder emails to employees.

5. Save.

Chapter 8: Inventory

How to Set Up Inventory Tracking

QuickBooks has everything you need to manage your inventory. Inventory tracking allows one to receive timely notifications about buying or selling.

To enable inventory tracking, follow these steps:

1. Go to "Settings" and select "Accounts and Settings".
2. Select "Sales".
3. Select "Edit" in the product and service section.

4. Click on the "Show Product or Service" column on sales forms.
5. Click on both track quantity and price, and track inventory quantity on hand.
6. Select "Save" and then "Done."

Keep a record of what sells. You can track when your inventory product is sold once set up. There are two ways to look through your track.

1. If you expect to be paid later, create an invoice.
2. If a customer pays on the spot, include a sales receipt.

The invoice or sales receipt reduces the amount on hand in QuickBooks.

To Check What's on Hand and Order as You Work

1. Click on the quantity of the item you entered to see more.
2. QuickBooks will notify you when items are running low or out of stock if you also set a low stock alert.

To Check Low Stock

1. Go to the "Sales" menu, then click "Products and Services".

2. At the top, you will see if you are out of stock or have low stock.

Restocking Your Inventory

When it's time to restock, you can use QuickBooks to order stock and keep track of what you've received from suppliers and what's on order. The quantity on hand will automatically increase due to the number of products you receive.

To create and send a purchase order, follow these steps:

1. Select "Sales".
2. Click on "Products and Services".
3. Select "Out of Stock". Do not use any other filter to reorder low-stock and out-of-stock items from the same supplier.
4. Select the product at the top of the list. You will see a dropdown menu above the list of products.
5. Select the "Batch" action, then reorder. It will create a purchase order for one supplier.
6. Complete all the required information on the purchase order.
7. Select "Save" and then "Send".

Tracking What You've Received from The Vendor

The two methods for tracking items received from the supplier are described below.

1. If you intend to pay later, create a bill from a purchase order.
2. If you paid cash on the spot, make a cheque or expense.

This will notify QuickBooks of what was restocked, and the number of items received will increase the quantity in QuickBooks.

How to Create Categories and Subcategories

Grouping items in QuickBooks help to organize products and services in QuickBooks.

Creating A Category

Categories are used to group items/products of the same type together. Subcategories can be created if you want to be more specific.

1. Go to the "Sales" menu.
2. Select "Product and Services".
3. Select "More" and then "Manage Categories".

4. Select the "New Category", then enter the category's name. If you are needed to create subcategories, select the "Subcategory Box" and then the "Main Category".
5. Click on "Save".

Categorize Products and Services

When you add a new inventory product, service, or non-inventory item, you can add it to a category by selecting it.

If you have uncategorized items, the instructions below will show you how to categorize them.

1. Go to the "Sales" menu, then select "Product or Services".
2. Find the product or service to categorize.
3. Select "Edit" on the action column.
4. Select the category that fits the terms or add a new one to create a new one.
5. Click on "Save" and close

How to Add Products Manually

1. To add inventory items, turn on the inventory tracking
2. Add your product's name and category. Once every setting is in place, you can add a product.
3. Go to "Sales", then "Products and Services".
4. Click on "New" or "Additional Product and Services".

5. Select "Inventory".
6. Add a name or category of what you are tracking.
7. Select the unit from the unit dropdown.
8. Select the category.

Adding Product's Quantity, Reorder Point, and Inventory Asset Account

1. Add the available product, followed by the date you started tracking that quantity.
2. You can add a reorder point to get alerts if it is time to reorder.
3. Select the "Inventory Asset Account" and click on "Inventory Asset". QuickBooks uses this account to track the inventory value.

Adding Product's Sales, Tax, and Purchasing Details

1. Add your product's description on the sales form. This will reflect on customers' invoices, sales receipts, and other forms.
2. Add the unit price followed by the sales price.

3. Select the "Income Account" and find the account you use to track you sell.

4. Choose the "Inclusive of the Tax" option if required or essential.

5. Select the "Tax Category" and how the item should be taxed. If you do not see this, set up the sales tax on QuickBooks

6. Add your product's description on the purchase forms. It will show on bills, purchase orders, and other forms you send to suppliers.

7. Add the product's cost. If it changes, you can still enter the latest price when buying products.

8. Scroll down and select "Cost of Goods Sold" from the expense account.

9. Select the "Inclusive Purchase Tax", if required.

10. From the "Purchase Tax", select the applicable purchase tax.

11. Add "Reverse Charge".

12. Select a preferred supplier.

13. Select advance options.

14. Add a category for what you are tracking.

15. Select "Save" and then close.

How to Add A Spreadsheet of Products

QuickBooks financial management software includes options for running spreadsheet data within the QuickBooks portal.

QuickBooks can import worksheets saved in Excel spreadsheet format directly into the program.

Add a spreadsheet as shown below:

1. Create an Excel Data Wizard and place it in areas like customers, suppliers, and goods.
2. Create a spreadsheet in Excel format and utilize the transfer wizard to finish the operation.
3. Save the spreadsheet.
4. Enter the data for the spreadsheet. A client information spreadsheet could include contact, account, and credit information. It also provides the product name, wholesale and retail pricing, and reorder information.
5. Create the spreadsheet as usual.
6. Save the spreadsheet in Excel. For example, to save Open Office Calc in Excel format, click "Save".
7. Choose "Other Format" to get a list of available formats. Choose the "Microsoft Excel" format.
8. Click to "Save".

Uploading a Spreadsheet to QuickBooks

1. Open the "File" tab in QuickBooks.

2. From the utility menu, choose "Import", then "Excel Files".

3. Go to the place where you stored the spreadsheet, then choose the customer, supplier, or product category that belongs to it.

4. Select the spreadsheet and click "Okay" to open it in QuickBooks as a blank, prepared Excel spreadsheet.

5. Copy and paste data from your spreadsheet into this QuickBooks spreadsheet.

6. One column at a time, paste data from your spreadsheet into QuickBooks, and select "Add My Data Now".

7. To begin the transfer, save the spreadsheet to your computer. After the transmission, you may choose to delete the stored file.

8. When the transfer is complete, a message box will appear to link to the spreadsheet's destination in QuickBooks, such as the Vendor Center for a Vendors spreadsheet.

9. Examine the QuickBooks file where you transferred data. You might see it on the Customer Center's work tab if you transferred a customer spreadsheet.

Chapter 9: Insights and Reports

How to Customize Reports

Reports contain a wealth of information about the business. Reports can be customized in a variety of ways, including:

- Filter them to show only certain accounts or customers.
- Format the layout so that the correct data appears in the correct place.

Types of Financial Reports in QuickBooks

- Balance Sheet
- Profit and Loss
- Cash Flow

Running A Report

1. Go to "Reports".
2. Find and open a report.
3. Adjust report date by using the basic filters on the report.
4. Select "Customize" in the top right-hand corner of the page.
5. This will open the customization menu automatically.

Customize A Report

Multiple filters can be used to customize a report; many reports have a set of filters, and some are only available on specific reports.

What can be changed:

1. Rows or Column section: This is accomplished by specifying which rows and columns appear on the report.
2. Select the customers, suppliers, accounts, and products that appear on the report in the Filter section.
3. Change the reporting period, accounting method, and the number of formats in the general section.

Saving Custom Reports

1. Select "Customization".
2. Give your report a name.
3. Select "Save".

How to Customize A Report for Profit and Loss Account

1. Click on the report's menu
2. Choose the "Report Center".
3. Select the "Standard" tab bar.
4. Under the dropdown list, select "Company and Financials".
5. Choose one of the profit and loss reports and click "Run".
6. Once the profit and loss reports are displayed on the screen.
7. Click the "Customize Report" bar on top of the screen.
8. Under the customize report window, you can make any changes you want. For example, report basics like the dates, apply filters, font size, font color, and many more.
9. Click "Okay".

Managing Customized Reports

1. Go to "Reports" and select the "Custom Report" tab.
2. Find the group on the list.
3. Select "Edit" in the "Action" column for the report you want to delete.
4. Click "Delete".

How to View Profit and Loss

Profit and Loss Account

A QuickBooks report summarizes your revenue and costs over a specific period, such as a month, quarter, or year (in the case of a corporation). It provides a high-level overview of the net profit or net loss for the time under consideration.

An accrual-basis (A) profit and loss statement is a more accurate predictor of profitability than cash flow because it includes income and costs that you own or owe regardless of whether money changed hands in the transaction. For example, even if you have not yet paid for the items used in the job, the materials in each task reduce your net income. This provides a much better match between revenue and costs than cash flow.

Sample Profit and Loss Report

Paul's Plumbing
PROFIT AND LOSS
January - December 2021

		TOTAL
▾ Income	A	
Sales		2,234.00
Services		4,025.00
Total Income		$6,259.00
▾ Cost of Goods Sold	B	
Cost of Goods Sold		750.00
Supplies COGS		1,000.00
Total Cost of Goods Sold		$1,750.00
GROSS PROFIT		$4,509.00
▾ Expenses		
6100 Advertising Expense		120.00
6115 Bank Service Charges	C	48.00
Vehicle Expense		2,750.00
Total Expenses		$2,918.00
NET OPERATING INCOME		$1,591.00
▾ Other Income	D	
Late Fee Income		150.00
Total Other Income		$150.00
NET OTHER INCOME		$150.00
NET INCOME		$1,741.00

Profitability

The first section summarizes the revenue generated by selling items and services over a specific period. In 2021, Paul's Plumbing had a total revenue of $6,259.

The Value of Goods Sold

The second section goes over the costs of purchasing or manufacturing everything on offer.

Operating costs

The third section goes over the firm's non-COGS costs for the year. Paul's 2020 expenses came to $2,918. Net operating income is the difference between gross profit and operating expenses.

Other sources of revenue/expenses

The final section includes revenue and costs unrelated to the business's normal operations. Customer late fees were classified as other revenue by Paul's Plumbing. Net income, also known as profit, is calculated by adding net operating income to any other revenue and subtracting costs.

How to Create a Profit and Loss Statement in QuickBooks

In QuickBooks, the income statement may be generated in four simple stages.

1. In the left menu, click "Reports".
2. In the "Business Overview" section, click "Profit and Loss".
3. By scrolling up, you can view and modify the profit and loss report settings.
4. Select "Customize" to further personalize the report.
5. Click an email, print, or export the Profit and Loss Report in the report's top right corner.

How to Plan Your Cashflow

This report summarizes the net amount of cash and cash equivalents moved into and out of business.

Cash Flow Planner

The Cash Flow Planner is a valuable tool for forecasting your company's cash flow, cash outflows, and cash inflows. It examines your financial history to forecast future cash-in and cash-out transactions. Furthermore, you can add or edit future events to see how different changes affect your cash flow.

Changes to events in the planner have no impact or update on your books. This enables the owner to make sound financial decisions regarding saving, spending, borrowing, and transferring funds. Among these considerations are:

- What exactly is forecasting, and how does it function?
- What information does this report contain?

The cash flow planner chart forecasts expected income and spending by analyzing previous data from your QuickBooks Online-linked bank accounts. This category includes transactions that are both classified and unclassified. Furthermore, you can manually incorporate data to forecast cash flow by adding future events.

The cash flow planner graphic does not include the following elements:

- Credit card transactions
- Trust fund transactions
- Manually entered transactions into QuickBooks
- Files with multi-currency support

N/B: If the bank account is closed, the data on the graph is lost.

To Add an Event

1. Select the "Add Event" button.
2. Choose "Money In" for income transactions and "Money Out" for transactions involving expenditures.
3. Assign the event/service a name, set a price, and click "Continue".
4. Pick an event date.
5. When finished, click "Save".

To Edit or Delete an Event

1. Select and open an event.

2. Change the date, merchant name, and amount, or switch between cash inflow and cash outflow.

3. Select "Save" after making the changes.

All events have different labels:

- Prediction – QuickBooks predicts money in and money out events based on your financial history. These are denoted by a special icon.

- An invoice, a sales receipt, a bill, an expense, a paycheck,, and transactions entered into QuickBooks.

- Your regular accounting does not account for planned, money in, and money out events that you manually enter into the planner.

How to Create A Cash Flow Statement

1. Click the "Reports" menu
2. Choose "Statement of Cash Flows".
3. Choose "Standard".

How to Use the Cash Flow Planner

A cash flow planner is a tool that forecasts future cash flow in and out of your business based on historical data.

Here are the steps on how to use the cash flow planner:

1. In the "Navigator" tab, select the "Cash Flow" menu
2. Choose "Planner".

3. To configure your planner, implement the on-screen instructions.
4. Once the planner is set up, select the date filters to set the forecast range.
5. Select the "Cash Flow In and Out" and "Cash Balance Filter" to filter the list.
6. Click the bar and drag it across the chart to a specific date.

How to Edit and Delete Items in Cash Flow Planner

1. In the "Navigator" tab, select the "Cash Flow" menu.
2. Choose the "Planner" tab
3. Select items for editing or deletion.
4. If you are editing an item, make the necessary changes you want to make, then click "Okay" to save.
5. Suppose you are deleting an item. Select "Delete".

How to View Cash Inflows and Outflows

1. In the "Navigator" tab, select the "Cash Flow" menu.
2. Click the "Overview" tab.
3. Choose view to see open invoices and bills that generate cash, or view reports to see a summary of all unpaid invoices and bills.

How to Forecast

1. In the "Navigator" tab, select the "Cash Flow" menu
2. Choose "Planner".
3. Select the "Add Event" button
4. If it is income, select "Money In". If it is an expense, select "Money Out".
5. Print the name and enter an amount in the detail area, then click "Continue".
6. Select the date the event will occur.
7. Click "Save".

How to Adjust the Forecast

1. Choose "Update" at the top of the screen to view a list of past-due bills and invoices.
2. Select the new expected date and update every transaction you want to adjust.
3. Click "Okay".

Chapter 10: Mobile App

How to Send A Quote Using the App

QuickBooks Online is compatible with iPad, Android, and iPhone, allowing you to access your business information no matter where you are.

First, download the QuickBooks mobile app from iTunes or Google Play, depending on whether you have an iPhone or Android.

1. Log in to your QuickBooks using your username and password.
2. Use your QuickBooks details to sign into the app. The display on your device will be like that on the browser.

3. To create quotes, click on the "Plus" sign, then select "Quotes".

4. Select the customer and input the relevant information for the quote.

5. Email the quotation to the client.

6. The customer accepts the quote by signing on the iPhone or Android phone screen. This is done by clicking on the "Get Signature."

7. The customers will use their fingers or stylus to sign on the screen.

8. Click "Done" to save the quote updated. The signature captured will be saved as an attachment to the customer quote.

How to Send an Invoice Using the App

1. Open your mobile up and go to the "Shortcut" menu.

2. Select "Invoices" and then select the "Add New Invoice" near the bottom of the screen

3. In the first field, select the customer or project you are invoicing. If it is a new customer, select "Add" near the bottom of the screen.

4. If you choose an existing customer, you can either assign a new invoice number or leave it blank, and the QuickBooks

mobile app will assign a new invoice number in the sequence.

5. Depending on how you configure QuickBooks, today's date will be displayed automatically.

6. Next, select "Add Product or Service". The app will display the list of products and services you are dealing with.

7. Enter the quality and rate you want to appear on your invoices.

8. Enter the applicable tax code for the product.

9. Select "Add" upon completion of product or service update, after which an invoice will display.

10. Select "Save" after inputting all the required details, and you will notice a confirmation that an invoice has been created.

Sending an Invoice Using A Mobile App

1. Select "Send Invoice".

2. QuickBooks will retrieve the customer's email address and display the subject line and email message to customize if desired. You can see the invoice preview that customers will see if they open the email by scrolling down.

3. When you press the send button, you will see the invoice status and the date it was sent. The status will be updated

when the customer views the Invoice. You will also receive payment and deposit updates if you have a payment setup, and your bank is linked to a QuickBooks account.

How to Use Receipt Capture

1. Sign in QuickBooks on your android phone or iPhone using your online user ID and password once you are signed in.
2. Go to "Menu".
3. Tap on "Receipt Capture", and it will automatically open the camera. Take a photo of your receipt or bill.

4. Select "Use this photo" once you are satisfied with the receipt captured. You will receive a notification that the receiver has been uploaded on your phone.

5. Go to your QuickBooks Online.

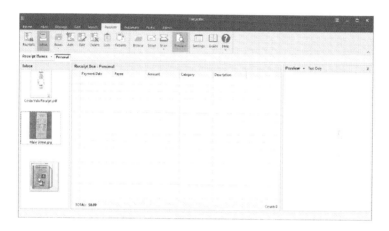

6. Select "Banking" and click on "Receipts".

Here is what you should do if QuickBooks discovers one or more transactions that match your submitted receipt or bill:

1. Click a receipt that will provide a list of the transactions that correspond with it.

2. Select the transaction you wish to associate with the receipt or the bill.

When a receipt or bill does not have a label next to the amount, it simply means QuickBooks could not locate an existing transaction that matches it. You can only create a new transaction using your receipt or bill as the basis.

1. Select the receipt or bill.
2. Create an expense or bill.

If the Receipt or Bill Has Missing Information

This indicates that QuickBooks does not extract all necessary information from a receipt or bill and requires additional data or specifications before issuing a bill.

1. Select the receipt or bill to update.
2. Select "Save the Receipt" or bill from the dropdown menu.
3. Create an expense, often known as a bill, for your company.
4. Visit the "Reviewed" page to see a list of all the receipts and invoices that you have entered your books.

Chapter 11: Bills and Expenses

How to Manage Expenses

If expenses have been paid in full, they should be recorded. Bills should be included if you plan to pay them off later.

Since you've already paid for them, you can change the costs you've entered into QuickBooks at any time. Any changes you make will be reflected in the invoice you send them if you choose to charge.

1. Go to "Expenses".
2. Find the expense you want to edit.
3. Select "Edit" or view in the "Action" column.
4. Update the transaction as required.

5. Select "Save" and close.

How to Record Cheques

Any expense can be paid with a check and tracked using expense accounts and non-stock, service, or charge items.

1. From the navigator, click the "Banking and Credit Cards" tab, then click "Cheques" or from the "Chart of Accounts" window, select the "Activities" menu, then choose "Write Cheques".
2. In the "Bank Account" field, choose your current account.
3. In the "Pay the Order of," choose from the dropdown list.
4. Enter the amount in the cheque.
5. Input the address and memo fields.
6. Edit items that are displayed from your purchase order or enter new ones.
7. To enter shipping charges and any other expenses not associated with any one item, click the "Expenses" tab, enter each charge, and connect it with the correct expense account.
8. Record the cheque.

Recording A Cheque

How to write a cheque on an "Income by Customer Summary" report:

1. Click "Banking" at the menu bar and select "Write Checks."
2. Select the appropriate bank account.
3. Select a "Payee" in the pay to the order.
4. Filter the date and the cheque number correctly.
5. Select the "Expense Account", then input the amount at the "Expense" Tab.
6. Click "Save" and close.

Printing A Cheque

1. From the "File" menu, choose "Print Form", and then choose "Print Cheques".
2. From the bank account dropdown list, choose the current account that contains the cheques you want to print
3. Check that the number in the first cheque number field matches the first number on your printer's cheques.
4. Select the cheques you want to print.
5. Click "Okay".
6. To print duplicate copies of vouchers cheques, input two in the number of copies field, then click "Print".

How to Delete A Bill

You can void or delete a cheque from the "Cheque" page so that you can review the "Informa" in the original transaction.

1. Go to "Expenses".

2. On the Expenses tab, select "Filter".

3. In the "Type" field, select "Cheque".

4. Select the date range in which the cheque was received and select "Apply".

5. To open the Cheque list screen, select the cheque to void from the "Expense Transactions" list.

6. Select "More" and select "Void" from the menu.

7. Click the "Yes" option to confirm the voiding of the cheque.

Voiding A Cheque Without Opening the Transaction

You can void a cheque from the Expense Transactions list without opening the transaction.

1. Go to "Expenses".

2. In the "Expense Transactions" list, search the cheque to void.

3. Select "Void" from the "View or Edit" on the dropping-down menu.

4. Select "Yes" to confirm that you want to void the cheque.

How to Delete an Expense

1. Go to "Expenses".
2. Find the expense you want to delete.
3. Select the "View or Edit" dropdown in the Action column
4. Select "Delete".
5. Click "Yes" to confirm transaction deletion.

How to Set Up Bulk Payments

1. Go to "Charts of Accounts".
2. Select the bank account you will be making payments from.
3. Once you have selected the bank account, click on the account history, and select "Edit".
4. A new field called "Create Batch Payment" will be displayed at the bottom of the screen. Select the field.
5. Enter your bank details; some banks might also need a direct entry user ID. If it is required, add the entry.
6. Click "Save".
7. Go to the "Suppliers" tab.
8. Select the supplier you need to pay.

9. Record the details of the supplier you intend to pay by clicking on the edit button next to the supplier name.

10. Select "I create batch payment box."

11. Fill in the account name and number.

12. Click "Save".

13. Click on the "Add Button" at the top of the screen and select pay bill. Add amount to be paid and mark to pay.

14. Click on "Create a Bulk Payment".

15. Save the file.

How to Record A Cash Expense

Expenses: An expense is the cost of operations that a company incurs to generate revenue during its operations. If a business meets the IRS guidelines, it can deduct tax-deductible expenses on its income tax returns. Accountants record expenses using one of two methods: cash or accrual.

Recording an Expense in QuickBooks

1. Select "Add New".

2. Select "Expenses".

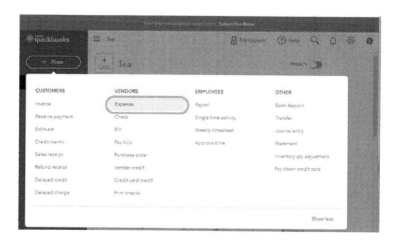

3. Select the supplier in the "Payee" field. The payment section also accounts for transactions made via bank for easy access and retrieval.

4. Input the date for the expense in the "Payment Date Area."

5. Choose the payment method for the expense in the "Mode of Payment" field. Enter the expenditure information in the "Category Details" section. Select the cost account you use to monitor spending transactions from the "Category" selection. Then, write a description for it. You may also insert items and services in the item details box to categorize the expenditure.

6. Enter the taxable amount.

7. Select the "Billable" option and input the customer's name in the "Customer" field.

8. When finished, choose "Save" and exit.

9. The "Memo" field also accepts notes. These show on reports and in the account history. If you utilize expenditure vouchers, choose "Print" to get a printed copy.

How to Manage Bills

Bills: This is the amount of money you owe your suppliers.

There are two ways you can manage your bills,

- Pay your bills as soon as you receive them. Write a cheque and assign their amounts to the appropriate expense account.

- Pay your bills later. You can enter the bills into your accounts payable account and set a reminder to remind you when they are due.

How to Enter Bills

1. From the activity's menu, click "Enter Bills" to display the enter bills window
2. In the "Supplier or Vendor" field, choose the vendor and the existing purchase orders that will be displayed
3. Select "Yes" to receive against one or more purchase orders.
4. On the "Open Purchase Orders" windows, click each purchase order containing items you have received and are billed for. Click "Okay".
5. Change the date of the bill. This is optional.
6. Enter the amount on the bill.
7. Input the reference number, terms, and memo fields as needed.
8. Click the "Items" tab. You can edit items entered from your purchase order or enter a new one.
9. To enter shipping charges or taxes not associated with any one item, click the "Expenses" tab, enter each charge, and associate it with the correct expense account

10. Use the "Split VAT or Add-on" buttons to change the VAT amount on each line of the detail area. This is also optional.
11. Record the bill.

How to Edit Bills and Payments

1. From the list's menu, go to the "Chart of Accounts" and click the "Accounts Payable" account.
2. Find the specific bill or payments.
3. Click "Edit" and make the changes required.
4. Click "Okay" to save.

How to Pay Bills

1. Click "Pay Bills" from the activity's menu to display the pay bills tab.
2. Choose the type of payment and the account from which you want to pay the bill
3. Fill in the optional fields in the pay bills window.
4. Select the bill to pay by ticking the checkbox.
5. To pay only part of the bill, enter the amount you would like to pay toward this billing in the amount paid column.
6. Record the payment.

How to Apply for Credit from A Vendor to Pay Bills

1. Click the "Purchases and Vendors" tab from the navigator, then click "Enter Bills".
2. At the top of the enter bills window, click "Credit".
3. Enter the amount of the credit.
4. Enter the expense accounts or customers to which you want to assign the credit
5. Use the "Split VAT or Add-on" buttons to change the VAT amount on each line of the detail area.
6. Record credit.

How to Enter Bill When You Receive It

1. Select the "Purchase and Vendor" tab from the navigator tab, then choose the "Receive Bill" icon.
2. Enter the vendor's name and press the tab in the item receipt window.
3. Click the item receipt connected with the bill and click "Okay".
4. Complete the reference #, terms, and memo fields.
5. Correct the amounts if necessary.

6. Make sure the amount shown in the amount field is the same as the total on the bill.

7. Record the bill.

How to Set Up Expense Settings

Setting Up Expenses Settings

1. Click on the "Add" icon or "Create Menu" from the top menu bar.

2. Select the "Expenses" option under supplier.

3. Open expenses.

4. Enter the supplier's name in the payee field and click "Add". You can either input the name of a person or a business. If there are multiple expenses in your transaction, you can leave this field blank.

5. Choose a payee.

6. Click on "Add Details" to input additional information like the type of currency and supplier or vendor, select "Save" if you choose to do it later.

7. Add details.

8. Choose a Payment Account from which the money of purchase will be deducted. Always put in mind that if you are using a debit card for the transaction, you must choose a Cheque Account, even if the card has a Visa on it.

9. Choose an account.

10. Input the date of purchase in the "Payment Date" field.

11. Enter the date.

12. Select how you made the payment in the "Payment Method" field – by credit card, cheque, or cash.

13. Choose payment method.

14. Under "Account", you need to choose a category for the purchase you have made.

15. Choose a category. If you cannot find the appropriate category for any item, you can add a new category and amount by clicking on the "Add Lines" option.

16. Add Description.

17. In the "Amount" field, enter the amount of purchased item and, if applicable, add the appropriate tax in the "Tax" field.

18. Add Amount.

19. If you want to create another expense, click on "Save and New" or select "Save and Close" upon completion.

* Some options to consider that will assist you in tracking expenses before you Save and Close:

The Billable column appears if you have enabled the billable expense tracking feature. Mark the Billable column and enter the customer's name. You have the option of enabling this feature for specific clients. Go to "Accounts and Settings", then the "Expenses" tab to perform this option.

NB: If you received credit for an expense billed to a customer in the past, make sure to mention that customer on credit and check the Billable box as well. If this is not done, the customer will be charged for the expenses on the next invoice, and no credit will be issued.

- If you want to see an income or the expense report for each customer, you should run an income by Customer Summary Report.
- You should add a brief note or Memo in case you want it to be on reports that include the purchase or in the Account History.

How to Make Expenses Billable

To record billable expenses, turn on the billable expense tracking.

1. Click on the "Settings" menu.
2. Select "Account and settings."
3. Navigate to the Expenses tab.
4. Select "Edit" at the Bills and expenses section.

5. Press the "Show Items" table on expense and purchase forms.

6. Track expenses/items by the client.

7. Make expenses and items billable by setting up the Markup rate, Billable expense, tracking, Sales, tax charge, and Bill payment terms.

8. Select "Save."

9. Input a billable expense.

How to Charge A Client for A Cost

1. Click on "New".

2. Select the "Bill, Expense, or Check" transaction.

3. Choose a payee.

4. In the "Classification" section, choose the expenditure account.

5. Enter the expense's description and amount, then check "Billable".

6. In the client column, click the customer to charge.

7. Tick the "Tax" checkbox or specify a tax if you wish to charge tax.

8. Save and exit.

Expenses to Invoices

1. Link the chargeable expenditure to the customer's Invoice.
2. Select "New".
3. Select "Invoice".
4. Select the client for whom you made a chargeable expenditure. Add to invoice window opens.
5. Add the billable expenditure to your customer.
6. Save and exit.

Made in United States
Orlando, FL
23 June 2022

19076299R00059